EVEN IN THE GRIEF

Even In The Grief

Poems on Finding Hope in Ambiguous Loss

SARAH J. CARTER

Dedication

To my parents, for celebrating my creativity and believing in me as a writer.

Contents

Dedication   v

Preface   1

SHOCK

Reality   6

Shredded   7

Nevermore, Forevermore   8

Unspoken Prayer   9

Dreams   10

Intent & Presence   11

Fragments   12

Side Effects   13

RECKONING

If Grief Were a Stain   16

Falling Short   17

A Heavy Load   18

Untitled Loss   19

What Does Time Heal?   20

Seven Wounds   21

PERIPHERAL LOSSES

Ducks   26

Petal by Petal   27

A Faded Version   28

Call it Tragedy   30

Stop Signs   34

Bitter Deep   35

Season's Grievings   36

Blackout   37

Mother-Daughter   39

PERMISSION

Acceptance   42

Boulder   43

Resting in Peace   44

When You Get to Heaven   45

Multitudes   46

Contents ~ ix

Bitter Hope   47

In the Face of Grief   48

The Days You Didn't   50

A Message from the Author   51
About the Author   53
Notes   55

Preface

Grief is complicated. It's about pain but it's also about hope. It's about making sense of loss while also accepting the unthinkable. While grief is almost universal, ambiguous loss is a more unconventional experience.

Dr. Pauline Boss coined the term in the 1970s to refer to "'lack of information and closure that surrounds the loss of a loved one.'"[1] In short, ambiguous loss occurs when the context or cause of death is unclear.

Examples of ambiguous loss that Dr. Boss explored included:

- Unexplained disappearances
- Loss of contact due to divorce, adoption, estrangement, incarceration, or immigration
- Psychological loss caused by traumatic brain injury, dementia, or other chronic mental illness[2]

I would offer that death from overdose or reckless behavior could also be considered a form of ambiguous loss. In these cases, sometimes the intent is unclear, leaving the bereaved with unanswerable questions.

As a disclaimer, I want to emphasize the distinction between ambiguous loss and suicide. There is a lot of stigma around suicide and when the intent is clear, it is important to name the cause of death, without shame. However, there are also many incidents of people who died from reckless behavior where the intent is unclear. *Even In The Grief* speaks to these circumstances, as well as the wider experience of ambiguous loss, which can go far beyond Dr. Boss' list.

These free-verse poems speak to how difficult it is to get your bearings in grief when you don't know how to describe the loss. The collection invites you to acknowledge the complicated pain and gently journey towards hope. Not hope as you once knew, but hope that you fight for in spite of so many reasons not to.

The collection is divided into four sections: Shock, Reckoning, Peripheral Losses, and Permission. These sections and their poems both mirror and at times question the conventionally understood stages of grief.[3]

Shock explores the sting of first learning about the loss. As you read, you may find yourself experiencing shock again, but this time the poems will sit with you as a gentle companion to the sting. The poems validate how disorienting the shock is while also acknowledging the universality of the experience.

Reckoning explores how grievers try to bargain with the loss to explain it away or make sense of it. These poems invite us to acknowledge the strength and courage it takes to reckon with an unthinkable and ambiguous loss. Finding the words to explain and admit what we can't explain is an essential part of healing. Additionally, these poems explore preconceived notions of grief itself by both questioning and invoking the seven stages of grief.

Peripheral Losses explores secondary or adjacent losses we experience in grief, such as loss of the sense of self and loss of hope. It also explores how suddenly other people's grief hits closer to home. By exploring peripheral losses, I hope you will give yourself permission to acknowledge how grief has changed your view of both yourself and others. Admittedly, this stage can feel self-centered and unnatural; however, grief changes us. Acknowledging secondary losses can bring healing as it helps us to reorient ourselves with who we've become after loss.

Finally, *Permission* explores the process of accepting the loss, accepting the enduring pain, accepting what you cannot get back, and accepting the new person you are. These poems invite you to give yourself permission in your grief journey—both permission to enjoy life again and permission to continue carrying the grief. We have to give ourselves permission to grow through the grief, to let the grief change, and to keep on living. I would reject the idea of moving on or "getting over" a tragic loss. Neither framework reflects the many shades of gray we live in, nor the way grief and life can mutually coexist.

Just as grief takes many forms, so do these poems, offering both short and long-form pieces. The longer pieces reflect moments when grief propels us to hunt for explanations, while the shorter pieces speak to simple devastation. Just as grieving is a decidedly raw and unpretentious experience, the verses in this collection offer dressed-down but apt language.

As you read these poems, you may find familiar notions of hope and despair, even if you did not experience loss exactly as it's described in this collection. Those points of connection are real. So if a line captivates you, it is no less for you if your grief is due to other circumstances. Some of the most healing moments in my own grief journey have been finding I connect more deeply with people who have experienced many kinds of loss. While I would never wish such loss on anyone, I cherish these points of sincere connection. May you find comfort in these poems on your journey through grief.

Shock

Reality

I have replayed this story
Sitting in silence, eyes closed
In a daze on the tram
Right before bed
Once I wake
And as I stare into a blank page
Waiting for the words to arrest this reality
That I cannot accept

Shredded

And so here we are
Standing in the carnage of broken hearts
Fleshy pieces of love, hope, and devotion
Completely shredded

Nevermore, Forevermore

Today I lost you
And I've never loved you more

Unspoken Prayer

There are words I keep in
Though they try to escape

They are heavier than a building
Stronger than a river

And they echo to no end

Words that throb
Rocking back and forth

I will say anything but these words

I will not admit
That when I talk about how I loved you
What I really want to say is

"Please, come back."

Dreams

Last night I dreamed
You came back to hug me
And all at once
It broke me
Put me back together
And broke me again

Intent & Presence

You and
What you were thinking
What I never had and
What I will never have again

Fragments

I cannot keep my heart
From reaching for all the shreds
From straining to make itself whole
I cannot keep my heart
From chasing fragments

-Broken

Side Effects

Hands
Heart
Body

Empty
Broken
Heavy

Reckoning

If Grief Were a Stain

If grief were a stain, I would scrub and scrub and scrub. But it's not. It's a long, winding road. No amount of elbow grease gets me further along. I only progress when I practice daily attention to how I'm doing.

"How are we today?"

–I ask but I'm not prepared for
My answer

Falling Short

Everything I gave you
Was all that I had
And yet it was still not enough

They say if love could keep you alive
You'd still be here
—Or is that wrong
Because love let you choose

So here I am
And the only thing I feel
More than love

Is how much I hate
Your choice

A Heavy Load

I wasn't done giving you love
Won't you come back
So I can lighten this load
It's too much to carry
And anyway
It belongs to you

Untitled Loss

An accident means it was unplanned
Suicide means with intention

. . . Means you understood
. . . Means you were sick
. . . Means you are gone

It seems only two apply
So this loss is
Untitled

What Does Time Heal?

They will try to charm you with phrases like
"Time heals all wounds"

Sometimes time is cruel
Yet it also knows the shape of kindness

I do not know if time will help
But it is always there
In the days I count since it happened

A step ahead yet
Lagging behind

Like a coy firefly
Difficult to catch, difficult to keep
Never staying l o n g enough
To patch me up

Seven Wounds

They say there are seven stages of grief
Shock, denial, anger,
Bargaining, depression, testing, and
Acceptance
Naming each stage is empowering
And every piece of power is needed
In the face of grief
Which is a word I am tired of saying

If I could offer a synonym it would be
Gasp
Because the finality of death takes your
Breath
And then stuffs it back down your throat
That humbling realization that you still have
Lungs and life though
The glass on the picture frames is cracked
Memories bless even as they torment
And the sun in the sky mocks
The hurricane happening inside

Some call it stages of grief
As if they would be so kind to take turns
When rather they come all at once like
Rain, thunder, lightning, and wind
Sadness like water falling from the sky
Rising from the ground
And being flung through the air so that
Separating the elements is as
Impossible as
Separating the pain
From the love

These stages do not stay in line
And are more like seven bullet wounds
Than mere phases
More like being pulled in seven directions or
Seven voices speaking to me at once
The more I accept
The more I am in shock of my acceptance
I mitigate through bargaining, just to realize
The immensity of what I am bargaining with

And in those gentle moments when I test out hope
My soul soaks it up like a sponge and
Just as quickly spits it out like poison
Desperate for solace yet fighting to accept
How much I need it

An exhausting realization that sends me to sleep
But my subconscious continues

Dreams of losing them
Dreams of saving them

My soul pulling me towards two conflicting realities
And seven different stages

If I could add an antonym for grief
It would not be gladness
It would be
Simplicity
Because it's the complexity of grief
That costs

It doesn't just change memories of past
But robs those you stowed away for the future
While still demanding your present

It can't be shaken with one
Therapy session
One funeral, eulogy
Or poem

It's not one loss but many
Including the person you were before
Whose soul was not yet marked with
These seven wounds

Peripheral Losses

Ducks

Could I put all these losses in a row
Like ducks
And shoot them?
It burns to realize
Loss can never
Die

Petal by Petal

Mourn by peeling
Petal by petal
All that you thought would be
There comes a day when the flower is bald
Unrecognizable
Much like me

A Faded Version

I am a faded version of the woman
In the photos
Before I became the one for which
They send thoughts and prayers

I have never before needed
But still hated
So much help

I would give it if this were happening to a friend
–But this has happened to me

This loss is a demarcation of
The life I had before

The moment I lost not just a person
But a life that was lived entirely on
The assumption that
This type of thing
Doesn't happen to
People like me

People like me send thoughts and prayers
To *other* people

–But here I am receiving condolences
Not knowing who I once was
When I believed I could live life
Above the reproach of tragedy

Did I truly believe we were eternal?

Call it Tragedy

I cannot listen to stories of near-death experiences
Without playing back
The day you died with one *minuscule* detail
Going differently

If I just slightly adjust the chess pieces on the board
There are a thousand different moves that
Could have led to
You still breathing
And one perfect storm that
Took you away

And no matter the number of replays
I get the same outcome
Over and over again

I try not to call your death a suicide
Because we don't know what you were thinking

And I also try not to say that it wasn't a suicide
Because we don't know what you were thinking

I thought I'd need to know what to call this
In order to make any sense of it

But instead I just call it loss
Instead I call it tragedy
And that's enough for me

But what wasn't enough
Were the prayers I prayed the day you died
Somehow knowing you needed them

Everything I gave wasn't enough
And all of us are counting up
What that everything was

It feels like so much and so little
All at once

There are always words to take back
Calls we would have taken
Measures that now don't seem so extreme

Grief pounds over and over again
And I'd like to blame someone just to divvy out
The weight I can't handle

They say that hurting people hurt people
I guess you didn't realize
That you were a person too

I guess you didn't realize
The day you went
A thousand hands were reaching for you

And I try to picture that homecoming
Of heaven's open gates
I try to picture how we look to you now
From the sky

And I try to picture a word that
Signals something like
Going forward but not moving on

Because there is always this piece of my heart
That can feel the news
As brutally as it hit the first day

This loss has done many things to us
–Those left behind to make sense of the pieces
But one thing it won't do
Is take away my gratitude

I thank God you're at peace
–Though I had a better plan for that

I thank God I'm surviving and
I thank God I'm shedding the guilt I feel for
Living at all

Because I realize that if I sit on the bench
It doesn't mean you get to play
It just means that more people pay

I let myself be sad, but not every day
I tell this story, and I'll live to tell other stories too

You see this loss may have left me empty handed
But I've got open palms
Not clenched fists

Stop Signs

I see the emptiness in your face
How your pupils look like stop signs
Asking me to not ask
How are you today

-I've been there too

Bitter Deep

I have never lost a sister or a brother
But when you tell me that you lost yours
I have a muscle memory of
The sobs that come from the bitter deep
I'll never know them how you knew them
But I know the deep,
My friend, I know it too

Season's Grievings

Instead of a happy thanksgiving
I will wish you a warm one
With the comfort of a heavy blanket
Even if it can't cover all the places that hurt

I wish you a fragrant cup of hot tea
Even if what you really miss is their smell

I wish you to light a candle,
Not just for their life, but for yours

Because though the very blood in your veins
Runs towards grief
It runs nonetheless

Though you wish it were you in that box, not them
Your love is still here
It is the warmth that
Never dies

Blackout

There's loss
And then there's loss that makes you look
At every person you love differently

Suddenly feeling the need to try to reckon with
The question . . .

What if I lost them too?

. . . As if grappling with this in advance
Might lessen the pain

There is loss
And then there's loss that makes
Every breath
Shrill

Every new day
Startling

The sun rises and

Even in the grief
You're making a coffee

How strange the sunny morning
A few capricious clouds
On the day of loss

Your soul in a blackout of grief
While the sun still shines

Mother-Daughter

At Grandmother's nursing home
The residents sleep while
We're on night watch for her passing

She takes her final breath and
I watch my mother whimper
And she becomes not just my mom
But someone else's daughter

And I cringe to wonder
What that whimper will look like
On me one day

Permission

Acceptance

Allow heartbreak to come
Succumb to the grief
It will leave no strength to reach for pieces
Or rearrange events
And you will no longer be able to tell the difference
Between love
And acceptance

Boulder

Just a piece of me is still sad
A piece that is a boulder
I gladly drag around

Resting in Peace

They say you're at peace now
And I need a picture of that to hold onto
So I picture us on a Saturday morning
And on this Saturday, it's not the day you die
It's just another lazy morning in eternity
We talk, but not about much
Sun warming our faces
Resting in peace
Together

When You Get to Heaven

When you get to heaven
You will still have some questions

And that is how you will know
You are in the right place

I have asked God not to tell you
How much I love you

"Let me tell them myself," I pleaded
And I believe God will answer this prayer

When I come I am going to tell you—
And it's not possible you understand
Even from that side of eternity
How much I cannot wait

Multitudes

They say we grow around the grief
Which feels like a pounding wound

My bereaved soul is layered and cloaked in
Resilience I never wanted to know

Yet here I am
Beholding not just loss but love
Not just pain but strength
And I cannot skin the parts I want
From the souring apples

Is this what Whitman meant when he said
Multitudes?

Bitter Hope

I carry in my hope
A swirl of bitterness for
The courage I needed to muster
To believe in promises again

Now hope is always in spite of
It never again sits as it once did
So simple and bright

In the Face of Grief

In the face of grief
Sometimes the most healing thing
Is to eat breakfast

Sometimes the most healing thing
Is to sob with all of your body
To let the pain shake you

All that being strong before—resisting tears
Was just preparation for this moment
When the grief hits in full force
Shaking every cell

Sometimes the most healing thing
Is to dance
To do with your body what you know
You will one day feel again

Sometimes the most healing thing

Is to put on makeup and fix your hair
Because on the list of 1,001 things
You cannot control
Your appearance is not one of them
Will your cheeks shimmer?
Only you can decide

Sometimes the most healing thing
Is to not make a plan
To accept that you don't know what you'll want
Or need to do when the moment comes
To not respond to the deck of texts offering
"Let me know if you need anything"

Sometimes the most healing thing
Is to make a plan anyway
To create some structure that you can
Pour the batter of your soul into
Force yourself to make some coherent shape
Because while the certainty of the future may be
Gone

You can still plan a walk in the park

So you go for a walk
Not knowing if tomorrow you'll need to
Eat breakfast, dance, fix your hair, or sob . . .

Whatever you do, you know
It will surely be in the face of grief

The Days You Didn't

I question if it really is a better place
—And how unfair it was for you to leave

You, beyond life, and me
Counting each of your completed days
The sum should equal a beginning
Equals an end . . . equals . . .

An infinity of pain that
I translate into a brazen commitment to
Breathe and love and
Go on walks
And do every damn cherished thing that I still
Can do

-Living the days you didn't

A Message from the Author

Thank you for reading *Even in the Grief*. If this poetry collection spoke to you, please consider leaving a review of the book. Leaving a review on Amazon or Goodreads is one of the best ways you can support this book and help others find it.

May you continue to find hope, even in the grief.

Gratefully,

-Sarah J. Carter

Connect
Instagram: @sarahjcarterauthor

About the Author

Sarah J. Carter is an author and poet from Norfolk, Virginia. She's been a featured poet at Busboys and Poets in Washington, D.C. and her poetry focuses on grief, healing, mental health and love. Sarah was a student editor for the *Appalachian Review* while earning a B.A. in English with a focus on Creative Writing at Berea College. She also holds a Master's in Conflict Resolution from George Mason University. Sarah currently splits her time between New York City and Washington, D.C.

Notes

1.   ^ "What Ambiguous Loss Is and How To Deal With It," Cleveland Clinic, February 17, 2022, https://health.clevelandclinic.org/ambiguous-loss-and-grief/.
2.   ^ "What Ambiguous Loss Is and How To Deal With It," Cleveland Clinic.
3.   ^ Psychiatrist Elisabeth Kübler-Ross introduced the idea of the five stages of grief, which includes denial, anger, bargaining, depression, and acceptance. This framework was later expanded to include the stages of reconstruction and hope.